Cambridge English

Flyers 8

Answer Booklet

CAMBRIDGE
UNIVERSITY PRESS

University Printing House, Cambridge CB2 8BS, United Kingdom

Cambridge University Press is part of the University of Cambridge.

It furthers the University's mission by disseminating knowledge in the pursuit of education, learning and research at the highest international levels of excellence.

www.cambridge.org
Information on this title: www.cambridge.org/9781107695108

© Cambridge University Press 2013

This publication is in copyright. Subject to statutory exception and to the provisions of relevant collective licensing agreements, no reproduction of any part may take place without the written permission of Cambridge University Press.

First published 2013
8th printing 2015

Printed in Italy by Rotolito Lombarda S.p.A.

A catalogue record for this publication is available from the British Library

ISBN 978-1-107-67271-0 Student's Book
ISBN 978-1-107-69510-8 Answer Booklet
ISBN 978-1-107-69459-0 Audio CD

Cover design by Peter & Jan Simmonett
Produced by Kamae Design, Oxford

Cambridge University Press has no responsibility for the persistence or accuracy of URLs for external or third-party internet websites referred to in this publication, and does not guarantee that any content on such websites is, or will remain, accurate or appropriate. Information regarding prices, travel timetables and other factual information given in this work is correct at the time of first printing but Cambridge University Press does not guarantee the accuracy of such information thereafter.

Contents

Introduction	4
Test 1 Answers	6
Test 2 Answers	12
Test 3 Answers	19
Combined *Starters*, *Movers* and *Flyers* Thematic Vocabulary List	25

Introduction

The *Cambridge English: Young Learners* tests offer an elementary-level testing system (up to CEFR level A2) for learners of English between the ages of 7 and 12. The tests include three key levels of assessment: *Starters*, *Movers* and *Flyers*.

Flyers is the third level in the system. Test instructions are very simple and consist only of words and structures specified in the syllabus.

The complete test lasts about one hour and a quarter and has the following components: Listening, Reading and Writing, and Speaking.

	length	number of parts	number of questions
Listening	approx. 25 minutes	5	25
Reading and Writing	40 minutes	7	50
Speaking	approx. 7–9 minutes	4	–

Candidates need a pen or pencil for the Reading and Writing paper, and coloured pens or pencils for the Listening paper. All answers are written on the question papers.

Listening

In general, the aim is to focus on the 'here and now' and to use language in meaningful contexts. In addition to multiple-choice and short-answer questions, candidates are asked to use coloured pencils to mark their responses to one of the tasks. There are five parts. Each part begins with a clear example.

part	main skill focus	input	expected response	number of questions
1	the main skill focus in all five parts of the Listening test is listening for specific information of various kinds, e.g. numbers, describing people, etc.	picture, names and dialogue	draw lines to match names to people in a picture	5
2		form or page of notepad with missing words and dialogue	write words or numbers in gaps	5
3		picture sets and list of illustrated words or names and dialogue	match pictures with illustrated word or name by writing letter in box	5
4		3-option multiple-choice pictures and dialogues	tick box under correct picture	5
5		picture and dialogue	carry out instructions to colour, draw and write (range of colours is: black, blue, brown, green, grey, orange, pink, purple, red, yellow)	5

Reading and Writing

Again, the focus is on the 'here and now' and the use of language in meaningful contexts where possible. To complete the test, candidates need a single pen or pencil of any colour. There are seven parts, each starting with a clear example.

Introduction

part	main skill focus	input	expected response	number of questions
1	reading definitions and matching to words copying words	nouns and definitions	copy the correct words next to the definitions	10
2	reading sentences about a picture and writing one-word answers	picture and sentences	write 'yes' or 'no'	7
3	reading and completing a continuous dialogue	half a dialogue with responses in a box	select correct response and write A–H in gap	5
4	reading for specific information and gist copying words	gapped text with words in a box	choose and copy missing words correctly tick a box to choose the best title for the story	6
5	reading and understanding a story completing sentences	story, picture and gapped sentences	complete sentences about story by writing 1, 2, 3 or 4 words	7
6	reading a story copying words	gapped text and 3-option multiple choice (grammatical words)	complete text by selecting the correct words and copying them in corresponding gaps	10
7	reading and understanding a short text (e.g. page from diary or letter) providing words	gapped text	write words in gaps no answer options given	5

Speaking

In the Speaking test, the candidate speaks with one examiner for about eight minutes. The format of the test is explained in advance to the child in their native language, by a teacher or person familiar to them. This person then takes the child into the exam room and introduces them to the examiner.

Speaking ability is assessed according to various criteria, including comprehension, the ability to produce a prompt, appropriate and accurate response, and pronunciation.

part	main skill focus	input	expected response
1	understanding statements and responding with differences	two (one is the examiner's) similar pictures oral statements about examiner's picture	identify six differences in candidate's picture from oral statements about Examiner's picture
2	responding to questions with short answers and forming questions to elicit information	one set of facts and one set of question cues	answer and ask questions about two people, objects or situations
3	understanding the beginning of a story and then continuing it based on a series of pictures	picture sequence	describe each picture in turn
4	understanding and responding to personal questions	open-ended questions about candidate	answer personal questions

Further information

The topics, structures, words and tasks upon which the *Cambridge English: Young Learners* tests are based are comprehensively described in the Handbook, so teachers or parents can know exactly what to expect.

Further information about the *Cambridge English Young Learners* tests can be obtained from the Centre Exams Manager for Cambridge ESOL examinations in your area, or from:

University of Cambridge ESOL Examinations
1 Hills Road
Cambridge CB1 2EU
United Kingdom

Telephone: +44 1223 553997
Fax: +44 1223 553621

Email: ESOLHelpdesk@CambridgeESOL.org
www.CambridgeESOL.org

Test 1 Answers

Listening

Part 1 (5 marks)
Lines should be drawn between:
1 Paul and the boy in the red T-shirt, near the paper hat on the floor
2 Sarah and the little girl in the high chair, with a toy bear, and ice cream on her face
3 Sally and the blonde girl, with a present in her hands
4 Emma and the girl in a striped T-shirt, carrying glasses
5 Richard and the boy near the door, going to press the light switch

Part 2 (5 marks)
1 sugar 2 scones (correct spelling)
3 48/forty-eight (cakes/scones) 4 10/ten minutes 5 jam

Part 3 (5 marks)
1 diary – C – suitcase   2 plate – A – garden
3 drum – E – basement   4 rock – B – bottom of sea
5 box – G – cave

Part 4 (5 marks)
1 C   2 C   3 B   4 A   5 B

Part 5 (5 marks)
1 Colour the top of the empty table – blue
2 Colour the skirt of girl pushing the swing – red
3 Write 'Spoon' on the sign above the door
4 Draw spots on the dress of the woman drinking, and colour the spots – green
5 Colour the newspaper in the bin – grey

TRANSCRIPT Hello. This is the Cambridge Flyers Practice Listening Test, Test 1.

Part 1 Listen and look. There is one example.

[pause]

WOMAN: Whose party is this?
GIRL: It's Harry's.
WOMAN: Which boy is he?
GIRL: He's the one at the far end of the table. He's eating some pizza.

[pause]

Can you see the line? This is an example. Now you listen and draw lines.

[pause]

WOMAN: Who's that boy in the red T-shirt?
GIRL: That's Paul. He goes to my school.
WOMAN: Where's his paper hat?
GIRL: It's fallen on the floor, but he doesn't know it yet.

[pause]

GIRL: Sarah looks happy, doesn't she?
WOMAN: Is she the little girl in the high chair?
GIRL: That's right. She's got a toy bear in her hand.
WOMAN: Yes, and there's ice cream on her face!

[pause]

GIRL: Look at Sally!
WOMAN: She's whispering something, isn't she?
GIRL: No, I mean the other girl, the blonde one.
WOMAN: Oh, yes, I see. She's got a birthday present in her hands.

[pause]

Girl:	Have you met Emma?
Woman:	Is she the woman who's bringing the birthday cake in?
Girl:	No, not her, I mean the girl. She's wearing a T-shirt with stripes.
Woman:	Oh, yes, I see her. She's carrying some glasses to the table.

[pause]

Girl:	Look! That's my cousin Richard, near the door.
Woman:	I can't see his face.
Girl:	No. He's going to turn the light off now.
Woman:	Then someone is going to cut the cake.
Girl:	Yes, and they're all going to sing 'Happy Birthday'!

[pause]

Now listen to Part 1 again.

[The recording is repeated.]

[pause]

That is the end of Part 1.

[pause]

Part 2 *Listen and look. There is one example.*

[pause]

Woman:	Now everyone, listen carefully. Tomorrow we're going to cook something together.
Boy:	Oh, good. What do we need to bring?
Woman:	Please bring a big bowl.
Boy:	OK.

[pause]

Can you see the answer? Now you listen and write.

[pause]

Woman:	I want you to bring some other things from home. Please write them on a piece of paper now.
Boy:	Do we have to bring flour, Miss?
Woman:	No, you don't. We already have some. But I want you to bring sugar, butter and eggs.
Boy:	OK, Miss. What are we going to cook?
Woman:	They're called *scones*. They are a kind of cake.
Boy:	Do you spell that S-C-O-N-E-S?
Woman:	Yes, that's right.
Boy:	How many scones are we going to make?
Woman:	There will be enough to make 48, so everyone can take some home.
Boy:	How long does it take to cook them? An hour?
Woman:	No! It only takes ten minutes.
Boy:	Are they nice, Miss?
Woman:	Oh, yes! They're lovely when they're warm. You can eat them with jam.

[pause]

Now listen to Part 2 again.

[pause]

[The recording is repeated.]

[pause]

That is the end of Part 2.

[pause]

Part 3 *Listen and look. There is one example.*

[pause]

Mr West works in a museum. Sometimes people give interesting things to the museum. Where did the people find these things?

[pause]

Girl:	Where did you get all these interesting things, Mr West?
Man:	Well, people found them in all kinds of different places. Look at these butterflies. They're beautiful, aren't they? A man caught them in the jungle 50 years ago. He brought them to our city and gave them to us.

[pause]

Can you see the letter F? Now you listen and write a letter in each box.

[pause]

Girl:	This looks very old!
Man:	Yes, it is. Last year, a woman gave it to us. It was her grandfather's diary. He was a famous actor so we were very happy to have it in the museum. She found it in an old suitcase in his house.

[pause]

Man:	We have a beautiful old plate in the museum too. A man was working in his garden when he found it under some leaves. He took it to a police station and the police gave it to us.
Girl:	Wow! It's lovely!

[pause]

Girl:	That's big!
Man:	The drum? Yes! Perhaps it's the biggest in the world. Someone found it in the basement of an old college and gave it to us. A lot of people came to see it, but they can't play it!

[pause]

Girl:	And what's the oldest thing in the museum?
Man:	That's a good question, Sarah. It's this rock. It's a strange colour, isn't it? A boy

Test 1 Answers

brought it to me and said, 'You can have this. It comes from the moon, I think.' He was wrong because it comes from the bottom of the sea. But it's very interesting and students and teachers of science come here to look at it.

[pause]

GIRL: What's your favourite thing in the museum, Mr West?
MAN: It's this box. It's full of gold. Two hundred years ago, some pirates found it in a cave on an island. They brought it to London and sold it.
GIRL: And now it's in this museum! Wow!

[pause]

Now listen to Part 3 again.

[The recording is repeated.]

[pause]

That is the end of Part 3.

[pause]

Part 4 *Listen and look. There is one example.*

[pause]

What did Richard win in the competition?

[pause]

BOY: I won a competition at school today.
WOMAN: Excellent! What did you win – a book?
BOY: No. This time I won a CD.
WOMAN: Mmm. You don't look very happy.
BOY: Well, Mum, my CD player is broken – remember?

[pause]

Can you see the tick? Now you listen and tick the box.

[pause]

1 *What did Richard buy at the shop?*

WOMAN: Did you get those things from the shop for me?
BOY: Yes and no. I bought the envelopes you wanted, but they didn't have any paper.
WOMAN: And did you remember the dictionary?
BOY: Oh, sorry! I forgot it.

[pause]

2 *What homework has Richard got tonight?*

WOMAN: Have you got any homework tonight?
BOY: Well, I haven't got any math now.
WOMAN: Why not?

BOY: I did it on the bus. But I still have to read about a famous painter tonight, for art.
WOMAN: Your geography teacher never gives you any homework. Why is that?
BOY: He does sometimes, Mum ... but not this week.

[pause]

3 *Which of these is clean?*

BOY: I'm going to play football tomorrow morning, Mum.
WOMAN: Oh! You didn't tell me – your shorts are dirty.
BOY: Oh, Mum! I can still wear them. Is my football shirt clean?
WOMAN: No, I haven't washed that yet. But there are some clean socks in your cupboard.

[pause]

4 *How is Richard going to get to the football game?*

BOY: Can Dad take me to the game tomorrow?
WOMAN: He can't. We've got a problem with the car. Can you go by bike?
BOY: Yes. The game is early in the morning, and there isn't a bus at that time.
WOMAN: I know.

[pause]

5 *What job does Richard want to do?*

WOMAN: Well, Richard, perhaps one day you'll be a famous footballer!
BOY: Oh, Mum! I want to be a photographer. You know that!
WOMAN: Are you sure? When you were younger you wanted to be a pilot.
BOY: I know. But I feel different now.

[pause]

Now listen to Part 4 again.

[The recording is repeated.]

[pause]

That is the end of Part 4.

[pause]

Test 1 Answers

Part 5 *Listen and look at the picture. There is one example.*

[pause]

MAN: Look at that bird!
GIRL: It's stolen that woman's sandwich.
MAN: That's right. Can you colour the bird?
GIRL: Shall I colour it yellow?
MAN: Yes, that's fine.

[pause]

Can you see the yellow bird? This is an example.

Now you listen and colour and write and draw.

[pause]

1

MAN: Can you see the empty table?
GIRL: Yes, I can. There aren't any people sitting there.
MAN: OK. Just colour the top of it blue, but don't do the legs!
GIRL: All right. I've done it.

[pause]

2

MAN: Can you see the two children?
GIRL: Yes. Shall I colour the child on the swing?
MAN: No. Look at the child who's pushing the swing. Colour her skirt red.
GIRL: OK. I'll do that now.

[pause]

3

MAN: I'd like you to write something now. Can you see the café?
GIRL: Yes. There's a kind of board above the door.
MAN: That's right. Write the word 'Spoon' in the space.
GIRL: All right.

[pause]

4

GIRL: Can I draw something next?
MAN: Yes, of course. Look at the woman.
GIRL: Which one? The one inside who's carrying some cups?
MAN: No, the one who's sitting with her family and drinking tea.
GIRL: What shall I draw?
MAN: Draw some spots on her dress and colour them green.

[pause]

5

GIRL: Can I colour one of the newspapers now?
MAN: OK. Colour the one in the bin.
GIRL: Shall I colour it grey?
MAN: Yes, that's fine. Look, you've finished now.

[pause]

Now listen to Part 5 again.

[The recording is repeated.]

[pause]

That is the end of the Flyers Practice Listening Test 1.

Reading and Writing

Part 1 (10 marks)

1 a journalist   2 factories   3 a bicycle   4 ice
5 hotels   6 a storm   7 a rainbow
8 post offices   9 a clown   10 a taxi

Part 2 (7 marks)

1 yes   2 no   3 yes   4 yes   5 no
6 yes   7 no

Part 3 (5 marks)

1 A   2 E   3 F   4 H   5 D

Part 4 (6 marks)

1 clothes   2 fell   3 drove   4 brave
5 chocolate   6 David has to go to hospital

Part 5 (7 marks)

1 car
2 King's Cross (station) (in London) // a/the station (in London)
3 (heavy) rucksack
4 a book (about/of dinosaurs) (out of/from his rucksack) // a dinosaur book (out of/from his rucksack)
5 Katy // Mark's (little/younger) sister (Katy)
6 map (of London) // London map
7 money (in his pocket)

Part 6 (10 marks)

1 There   2 Each   3 at   4 the   5 than
6 called   7 all   8 get   9 after   10 clean

Part 7 (5 marks)

1 for/on   2 telling   3 took   4 out
5 us (all)/everyone

Test 1 Answers

Speaking

Part	Examiner does this:	Examiner says this:	Minimum response expected from child:	Back-up questions:
	Usher brings candidate in.	Usher to examiner: **Hello, this is** (*child's name*)*.		
		Examiner: **Hello *.** My name's *Jane/Ms Smith*.	Hello.	
		What's your surname?	*Silver*	What's your family name?
		How old are you?	*ten*	Are you *ten*?
1	Shows candidate both **Find the Differences** pictures.	Now, here are two pictures. My picture is nearly the same as yours, but some things are different.		
	Points to the clouds in each picture.	For example, in my picture there are three clouds, but in your picture there are four. OK?		
	Describes things without pointing.	I'm going to say something about my picture. You tell me how your picture is different.		1. Point at relevant difference(s). 2. Repeat statement. 3. Ask back-up question.
		In my picture, there's a black swan on the lorry.	*In my picture, there's a white swan.*	What colour is the swan?
		In my picture, two children are playing with a fire engine.	*In my picture, they're playing with a rocket.*	What are the two children playing with?
		In my picture, there's a helicopter on the left.	*In my picture, the helicopter's on the right.*	Is the helicopter on the left?
		In my picture, the tables outside the café are round.	*In my picture, the tables are square.*	Are the tables round?
		In my picture, a girl with curly hair is buying a rucksack.	*In my picture, she's buying a suitcase.*	What is the girl buying?
		In my picture, it's quarter past eleven.	*In my picture, it's quarter to twelve.*	What time is it?
2	Shows candidate both **school** information pages. Then points to candidate's information page.	Peter and Sally both go to different schools. I don't know anything about Peter's school, but you do. So I'm going to ask you some questions.		
	Points to the boy on candidate's information page. Asks the questions.	What's the name of Peter's school? Where is it? How many children are there in the school? Who's his English teacher? What's Peter's favourite lesson?	(It's) *Hill School.* near the *bank* (There are) *700.* (It's) *Mr Black.* (It's) *history.*	Point at the information if necessary.
	Points to the girl on candidate's information page.	Now you don't know anything about Sally's school, so you ask me some questions.		

* Remember to use the child's name throughout the test.

Test 1 Answers

Part	Examiner does this:	Examiner says this:	Minimum response expected from child:	Back-up questions:
	Responds using information on examiner's information page.	It's called City School. There are 650. It's opposite the cinema. She loves geography. It's Mrs Brown.	*What's the name of Sally's school? How many children are there in the school? Where is it? What's her favourite lesson? Who's her English teacher?*	Point at information cues if necessary.
3	Shows candidate **Picture Story**. Allows time to look at the pictures.	These pictures tell a story. It's called 'Emma sees her favourite singer'. Just look at the pictures first. Emma's favourite singer is going to sing in the park tonight. Emma is saying to her parents, her brother and her grandma, 'Please can someone take me?' Now you tell the story.	*Emma's parents want to go to a restaurant tonight.* *Emma's brother wants to watch football on television.* *Emma's grandma is very excited. She wants to take Emma.* *Emma and her grandma are listening to the singer. They are both enjoying the music very much.*	1. Point at the pictures. 2. Ask questions about the pictures. Who is Emma asking now? What do Emma's parents want to do this evening? Who is Emma asking now? What does Emma's brother want to do? Does Emma's grandma want to take her to see the singer? What are Emma and her grandma doing now? Do they like the music?
4	Puts the pictures away and turns to the candidate.	Now, let's talk about the holidays. What time do you get up in the holidays? What do you do with your friends in the holidays? What do you do with your family? When was your last holiday? Tell me about your last holiday.	*(at) 9 o'clock* *play tennis* *go shopping* *(in) August* *We went to the sea. I played on the beach. I had fun.*	Do you get up at *9 o'clock*? Do you *play tennis* with your friends? Do you *go shopping* with your family? Was it in *August*? Where did you go? What did you do? Did you have fun?
		OK, thank you, *. Goodbye.	*Goodbye.*	

* Remember to use the child's name throughout the test.

Test 2 Answers

Listening

Part 1 (5 marks)

Lines should be drawn between:
1. Robert and the boy making the snowman, holding the snowman's arm
2. Katy and the girl standing on the ice
3. Michael and the man planting skis in the snow
4. Betty and the blonde woman pulling the sledge
5. Harry and the man skiing downhill, wearing green gloves

Part 2 (5 marks)
1. 8/eight (o'clock/am) // (0)8.00 (am)
2. (the) Harding (correct spelling)
3. insects
4. (a) snack/lunch // (some) food // snacks
5. (the) (school) uniform(s)/(the) school clothes

Part 3 (5 marks)
1. butterfly – G – in old suitcase   2. leaf – F – picture frame
3. stamp – H – old book   4. pen – C – tent   5. video – D – shelf

Part 4 (5 marks)
1 A   2 A   3 C   4 B   5 B

Part 5 (5 marks)
1. Colour the flag next to the man with the camera – green
2. Colour the planet with a ring – yellow
3. Draw a plate between the two rocks and colour it – blue
4. Write 'Wings' on the stripe of the rocket
5. Colour the bird in the cage – brown

TRANSCRIPT   *Hello. This is the Cambridge Flyers Practice Listening Test, Test 2.*

   Part 1   *Listen and look. There is one example.*

   [pause]

   GIRL: Look, Mr Swan! This is a picture that I took when I went for a holiday in the mountains in December. There's my brother, Richard!
   MAN: Which one's he?
   GIRL: The boy who's got the strange hat on. It looks like a tail. He's fallen over.
   MAN: I see. Was he OK?
   GIRL: Oh, yes!

   [pause]

   Can you see the line? This is an example. Now you listen and draw lines.

   [pause]

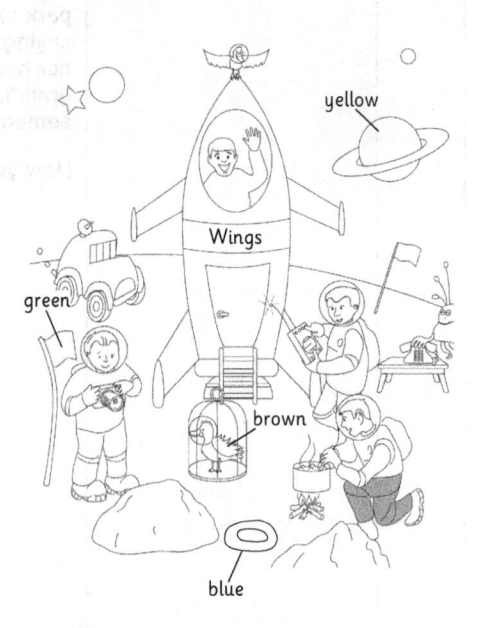

   MAN: Who are the two boys who are making the snowman?
   GIRL: I only know one of them – Robert. He's got an arm for the snowman in his hand.
   MAN: Is he someone in your family too?
   GIRL: No. I met him there. He stayed at the same hotel.

   [pause]

   MAN: Is that a lake on the right of the picture?
   GIRL: Yes, and there's my older sister, Katy.
   MAN: But isn't that a boy?
   GIRL: Yes, but look. The girl who's just standing on the ice! That's my sister. She isn't moving in this picture.
   MAN: Oh, I see now.

   [pause]

   MAN: And who's that? The person with the skis?
   GIRL: The woman who's lost her glasses?

Test 2 Answers

MAN: Not her. The man who's just put his skis in the snow.
GIRL: Oh, you mean Michael! He's a friend of my dad's. He came with us.
MAN: Oh.

[pause]

MAN: What a lot of snow!
GIRL: Yes! I had lots of fun there. We all did. Can you see the woman who's pulling the sledge? That's my mother. She's got blonde hair.
MAN: I see. What's her name?
GIRL: I call her Mum, but her first name's Betty.

[pause]

MAN: And who's the person who's skiing down the mountain … the one with the green gloves?
GIRL: That's Harry. He's another friend of ours.
MAN: Does he like going very fast?
GIRL: Yes, but he's not always very careful. He broke his arm last winter!
MAN: Oh dear!

[pause]

Now listen to Part 1 again.

[The recording is repeated.]

[pause]

That is the end of Part 1.

[pause]

Part 2 *Listen and look. There is one example.*

[pause]

WOMAN: Good morning, children! We're going to visit a museum next week. Do you remember? You need to tell your parents about it, so listen carefully.
BOY: Are we going to go there on the train, Miss Fish?
WOMAN: Yes. That's right, David. We'll all walk to the station from the school together that morning.
BOY: Great! It's going to be an exciting day!

[pause]

Can you see the answer? Now you listen and write.

[pause]

BOY: What time will we leave school, Miss Fish?
WOMAN: We have to leave here at eight o'clock. Sorry! I know it's early, but we'll have more time at the museum if we leave then.
BOY: Does it take a long time to get there?
WOMAN: Yes. But the museum is very good. You'll see.
BOY: What's the name of the museum, Miss Fish?

WOMAN: It's called the Harding Museum. Write that down, please.
BOY: Is that H-A-R-D-I-N-G?
WOMAN: Yes, that's the right way to spell it.
BOY: And what will we see there? Will it be paintings like last time?
WOMAN: No, we're going to learn about insects at the museum. We're going to look at some, draw some and find out a lot of things about them. It will be very interesting for you.
BOY: Wow! It sounds excellent! Can we buy our lunch there too?
WOMAN: No. There's no café there. So this is important. You must all bring a snack with you to eat at midday. Don't forget!
BOY: OK. And what must we wear that day? Can we wear jeans?
WOMAN: No, you're not in school that day, but you must still wear your uniform.
BOY: Oh …
WOMAN: You're going to have a very good day there, David. Don't forget to tell your parents all about it, children. Now open your math books, please. We've got lots of work to do this morning.

[pause]

Now listen to Part 2 again.

[The recording is repeated.]

[pause]

That is the end of Part 2.

[pause]

Part 3 *Listen and look. There is one example.*

[pause]

Emma has a lot of things in her treasure box. Where did she find each thing?

[pause]

MAN: Emma, look at this box! It's full of things. You don't need all these!
GIRL: I do, Dad! They're all important! Look, here's a ticket. I found it on a bus about a year ago. It's interesting because it's a different colour and it's from a different town.

[pause]

Can you see the letter B? Now you listen and write a letter in each box.

[pause]

MAN: But why do you want these things?
GIRL: I don't know. I just do! Look, this is good too. It's a butterfly. Mum saw it on a strange plant in a forest and took a picture of it 30 years ago on holiday. I found it in her old suitcase.

[pause]

13

Test 2 Answers

MAN: And what's this?
GIRL: Oh, that? It's an old leaf. It's a great colour, isn't it? Grandma gave me that last summer. It was in a picture on her wall in the flat. She didn't like it, but I did, so she took it out and gave it to me.

[pause]

GIRL: And this stamp is one of my favourite things! It's a hundred years old, Grandpa said. Look, it's red and it's got a queen's face on it. Grandpa and I found it inside the pages of a book. He gave it to me. He said I must be very careful with it.
MAN: Let me look at it … oh, yes! It *is* old.

[pause]

MAN: And whose is that?
GIRL: This little silver pen? Don't you remember? When we put Uncle Tom's tent up in the garden, we found it inside. You telephoned him about it. He said I can have it. It doesn't write, but I like it.

[pause]

MAN: And this?
GIRL: That's an old video. It's about finding a toy bear in a cupboard. But we don't play them now, do we? We only have DVDs. But in the future, someone will be very interested in this. It was on that high old shelf in the basement. I'm going to look after it. Then *my* children can take it to their history lessons!

[pause]

Now listen to Part 3 again.

[The recording is repeated.]

[pause]

That is the end of Part 3.

[pause]

Part 4 *Listen and look. There is one example.*

[pause]

What is Jack looking at on the computer now?

[pause]

WOMAN: Jack! Are you using the computer again? Are you playing games?
BOY: I am using the computer, Mum, but I'm reading some emails from my friends.
WOMAN: Well, be quick because I want to find a map of London. Jack?
BOY: Yes, Mum!

[pause]

Can you see the tick? Now you listen and tick the box.

[pause]

1 Why does the family want to go to London?

BOY: Can I go to London with you?
WOMAN: Yes, of course.
BOY: Why do you want to go there – to see your friends again?
WOMAN: No, I want to go to the theatre with Dad on his birthday! It's a secret. You mustn't tell him.
BOY: Great! Can we go to a restaurant there too?
WOMAN: We won't have enough money for that, Jack.

[pause]

2 What will Jack and his mother buy?

BOY: Have you bought Dad a present yet?
WOMAN: No, but I need to use the computer for that too. Shall we buy him a nice book?
BOY: He's got a lot of books already. Let's get him a DVD. You can buy those on the computer.
WOMAN: Good idea – or some golf balls?
BOY: No, Mum. He likes watching films more than playing golf.
WOMAN: OK!

[pause]

3 What must Jack find out about on the computer?

BOY: I need to find out about something on the computer too, later. It's for my homework.
WOMAN: About the artist? The one that your teacher told you about?
BOY: No. We did that last week. I need to know more about an important photographer. We looked at some of his pictures yesterday in art at school.
WOMAN: OK. I'll help you with that. And I want to find out about that famous singer. The one I heard on the radio yesterday.
BOY: Perhaps you can buy one of his CDs too!
WOMAN: Perhaps …

[pause]

4 What can Jack's best friend do well on his computer?

BOY: You know my best friend at school? The one who's very good on the computer?
WOMAN: Yes. Can he write very fast when he uses one?
BOY: No, but he can draw really well on it. He's excellent at that. I want to learn too.
WOMAN: Well, he can give you lessons, then! My friend at work writes music on hers. She's very good at that.

[pause]

Test 2 Answers

	5 *What's wrong with the computer now?*
Boy:	I've only got three emails now. Oh, Mum! The computer's stopped working.
Woman:	What's the matter with it? Has it got lots of lines on it or spots again?
Boy:	No, it's all black. What shall I do?
Woman:	Wait a minute. I'll come and look at it. Oh, computers! Sometimes I love them and sometimes I hate them!

[pause]

Now listen to Part 4 again.

[The recording is repeated.]

[pause]

That is the end of Part 4.

[pause]

Part 5 *Listen and look at the picture. There is one example.*

[pause]

Man:	Shall we colour some of this picture now?
Girl:	Yes. It's funny! Some astronauts are on the moon!
Man:	That's right! Can you see the astronaut who's cooking something on the fire?
Girl:	Yes. Can I colour his space trousers?
Man:	Yes, OK. Colour them orange.

[pause]

Can you see the orange trousers? This is an example.

Now you listen and colour and write and draw.

[pause]

1

Girl:	What else can I colour? One of the flags?
Man:	Yes! Good idea! Colour the one which is next to the man with the camera.
Girl:	OK. And can I choose the colour this time?
Man:	Yes, all right!
Girl:	I'll use green, then.
Man:	OK.

[pause]

2

Girl:	There are some planets in the sky.
Man:	Yes, there are. Colour the one next to the star. No, sorry, colour the one that's got a kind of ring.
Girl:	Which colour must I use?
Man:	Let's colour it yellow. Do you agree?
Girl:	Yes! That's my favourite colour.

[pause]

3

Girl:	And can I draw something on this picture too?
Man:	Yes. Draw a plate on the ground between the two rocks. Can you do that?
Girl:	Yes. I'll draw a small, round one. Shall I colour it too?
Man:	Yes, please. Make it blue.
Girl:	All right. I'll do that now.
Man:	Good.

[pause]

4

Man:	Would you like to write something in this picture too?
Girl:	Oh, yes. I like writing. What can I write?
Man:	The rocket hasn't got a name. We must give it one.
Girl:	OK. What name shall we write on it?
Man:	Write 'Wings' on it. That's a great name for a rocket. Write it in the stripe.
Girl:	All right. I'll do that now.

[pause]

5

Man:	We should colour one more thing now. How about the strange bird in the cage?
Girl:	All right. Did it come with the astronauts?
Man:	Yes. It came with them from our world. Make it red.
Girl:	Can I colour it brown? That's a better colour, I think.
Man:	Yes, that's fine.
Girl:	I've finished now.
Man:	Well done!

[pause]

Now listen to Part 5 again.

[The recording is repeated.]

[pause]

That is the end of the Flyers Practice Listening Test 2.

Reading and Writing

Part 1 (10 marks)

1 newspapers   2 an envelope   3 a hospital
4 scissors   5 a belt   6 a chemist's   7 shorts
8 a brush   9 pockets   10 a diary

Part 2 (7 marks)

1 no   2 no   3 yes   4 no   5 yes   6 no
7 yes

Part 3 (5 marks)

1 D   2 F   3 E   4 H   5 G

Test 2 Answers

Part 4 (6 marks)
1 job   2 decided   3 neck   4 treasure
5 clever   6 Fun at Grandma's

Part 5 (7 marks)
1 (some) photos/pictures/photographs
2 got up early   3 unhappy/sad   4 bats
5 (big) torch/flashlight
6 ((one of) the) (old) (rock) walls // a/the wall
7 (nice) (new) house // (own) home

Part 6 (10 marks)
1 called   2 in   3 of   4 get   5 are
6 at   7 for   8 Every   9 or   10 have

Part 7 (5 marks)
1 Uncle   2 to   3 were   4 there   5 said

Speaking

Part	Examiner does this:	Examiner says this:	Minimum response expected from child:	Back-up questions:
	Usher brings candidate in.	Usher to examiner: **Hello, this is (child's name)***.		
		Examiner: Hello *, my name's *Jane/Ms Smith*.	Hello.	
		What's your surname?	*Silver*	What's your family name?
		How old are you, *?	*ten*	Are you *ten*?
1	Shows candidate both **Find the Differences** pictures.	Now, here are two pictures. My picture is nearly the same as yours, but some things are different.		
	Points to the rucksack in each picture.	For example, in my picture the rucksack's closed, but in your picture the rucksack's open. OK?		
	Describes things without pointing.	I'm going to say something about my picture. You tell me how your picture is different.		1. Point at relevant difference(s). 2. Repeat statement. 3. Ask back-up question.
		In my picture, there are three camels.	*In my picture, there are two camels.*	How many camels are there?
		In my picture, there are some pyramids behind the tent.	*In my picture, there are some hills.*	Are there any pyramids behind the tent?
		In my picture, the man's wearing a small hat.	*In my picture, the man's wearing a big hat.*	Is the man wearing a small hat?
		In my picture, the bats are black.	*In my picture, the bats are brown.*	What colour are the bats?
		In my picture, I can see a lizard. It's got spots.	*In my picture, the lizard's got stripes.*	Has the lizard got spots?
		In my picture, the girl's waving.	*In my picture, the girl isn't waving.*	Is the girl waving?
2	Shows candidate both **sister's job** information pages. Then points to candidate's information page.	Sam has two older sisters, Daisy and Lucy. I don't know anything about Daisy's job, but you do. So I'm going to ask you some questions.		
	Points to the girl on the left on candidate's information page. Asks the questions.	What time does Daisy start work? Where does Daisy work? How does Daisy go to work? What is Daisy's job? Is the job interesting or boring?	*(at) half past 10* *(at a) café* *(She goes by) bike.* *(She's a) cook.* *(It's) boring.*	Point at the information if necessary.
	Points to the girl on the right on candidate's information page.	Now you don't know anything about Lucy's job, so you ask me some questions.		

* Remember to use the child's name throughout the test.

Test 2 Answers

Part	Examiner does this:	Examiner says this:	Minimum response expected from child:	Back-up questions:
	Responds using information on examiner's information page.	at a swimming pool She's a swimming teacher. at half past two by bus It's interesting.	*Where does Lucy work?* *What's Lucy's job?* *What time does she start work?* *How does she go to work?* *Is the job interesting or boring?*	Point at information cues if necessary.
3	Shows candidate **Picture Story**. Allows time to look at the pictures.	These pictures tell a story. It's called 'Where's the suitcase?' Just look at the pictures first. Mr and Mrs Green are going on holiday with their children but they've forgotten Mrs Green's suitcase. A man has seen the suitcase. Now you tell the story.	*A man has picked up the suitcase. He's putting it in his car.* *The family is at the airport. Mrs Green can't find her suitcase.* *The man's giving the suitcase to Mrs Green. She's very happy.* *The family is on the plane. But the suitcase isn't with them!*	1. Point at the pictures. 2. Ask questions about the pictures. What's the man doing? Where's the family now? Can Mrs Green find her suitcase? What's the man doing? Is Mrs Green happy? Where's the family now? Is the suitcase on the plane?
4	Puts the pictures away and turns to the candidate.	Now, let's talk about your bedroom. What colour are the walls? How many pictures are there in your bedroom? What's your favourite thing in your bedroom? What time do you go to bed? Tell me what you like doing in your bedroom?	*blue* *4* *(my) computer* *(at) 8.30* *I play computer games.* *I watch television.* *I listen to music.*	Are the walls *blue*? Are there *4* pictures? Have you got a *computer* in your bedroom? Do you go to bed at *8.30*? Do you *play computer games*? Do you *watch television*? Do you *listen to music*?
		OK, thank you, *. Goodbye.	*Goodbye.*	

* Remember to use the child's name throughout the test.

Test 3 Answers

Listening

Part 1 (5 marks)

Lines should be drawn between:
1 Helen and the woman with short hair, wearing a skirt with red stripes
2 William and the young man in the blue jacket, pointing to the suitcase
3 Fred and the man reading a newspaper, wearing shorts
4 Betty and the little girl holding a bear
5 Michael and the man in uniform, standing near the doors

Part 2 (5 marks)

1 Chopsticks   2 6/six (o'clock) (pm) // 6.00 // 18.00
3 Margie (correct spelling)   4 (a) cook // she is/'s a cook
5 (all) excellent

Part 3 (5 marks)

1 nurse – C – tent in field   2 artist – G – boat
3 dentist – F – wooden house in forest
4 tennis player – D – castle on top of hill
5 teacher – B – block of flats

Part 4 (5 marks)

1 B   2 A   3 B   4 C   5 C

Part 5 (5 marks)

1 Colour the empty glass on the table (on the right) – orange
2 Colour the octopus in the picture on the fridge – green
3 Write 'April' under '15th' on the date on the wall
4 Draw a plate on the upper shelf to right of the bowl and colour it – yellow
5 Colour the metal pedal bin near the cooker – blue

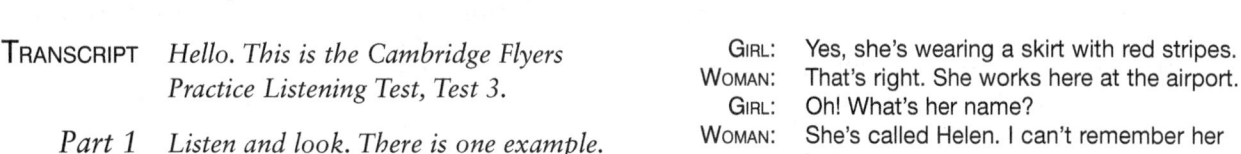

TRANSCRIPT	*Hello. This is the Cambridge Flyers Practice Listening Test, Test 3.*
Part 1	*Listen and look. There is one example.*
	[pause]
WOMAN:	Hello. I know some of these people.
GIRL:	Well, what's the name of that boy?
WOMAN:	Which boy?
GIRL:	The one who's looking up at the sky.
WOMAN:	That's David. He comes here every day to watch the planes.
	[pause]
	Can you see the line? This is an example. Now you listen and draw lines.
	[pause]
WOMAN:	Do you see that woman with short hair?
GIRL:	Yes, she's wearing a skirt with red stripes.
WOMAN:	That's right. She works here at the airport.
GIRL:	Oh! What's her name?
WOMAN:	She's called Helen. I can't remember her last name.
	[pause]
WOMAN:	And that's William. What's he doing?
GIRL:	Which one?
WOMAN:	The young man in the blue jacket.
GIRL:	Oh, he's pointing to his suitcase.
WOMAN:	But why is he doing that?
GIRL:	I don't know. Perhaps they're going to open it.
	[pause]
GIRL:	Is that Fred? The man who's reading a newspaper?
WOMAN:	Yes, that's him. He's wearing shorts today.
GIRL:	Is that strange?
WOMAN:	Well, he usually wears jeans.
	[pause]

Test 3 Answers

GIRL: That little girl looks unhappy.
WOMAN: Yes, she's pulling her mother's hand.
GIRL: No, not her. I mean the girl with the bear.
WOMAN: Oh, that's Betty. She's tired. She wants to get on the plane.

[pause]

WOMAN: Michael looks nice in his uniform.
GIRL: Is he the man with the moustache?
WOMAN: No, he's the man who's standing near the doors.
GIRL: Oh, yes, I see him.

[pause]

Now listen to Part 1 again.

[The recording is repeated.]

[pause]

That is the end of Part 1.

[pause]

Part 2 *Listen and look. There is one example.*

[pause]

BOY: Hello, Anna. Did you watch television yesterday?
WOMAN: Yes, I did, in the evening after work.
BOY: Good. Can I ask you some questions, please? I have to write something about television for my English homework.
WOMAN: Yes, of course.
BOY: How many programmes did you watch?
WOMAN: Three.

[pause]

Can you see the answer? Now you listen and write.

[pause]

BOY: Which was the best programme that you watched last night?
WOMAN: It was a film called 'Chopsticks'. It was very old, but I enjoyed it.
BOY: Mmm. I didn't see that. What time did it start?
WOMAN: At 6 o'clock. And it finished at half past seven. Then I had dinner, after that.
BOY: Were there any famous actors in the film?
WOMAN: Yes. Margie MacDonald. I love her films!
BOY: Oh. Can you spell her first name for me?
WOMAN: Yes. It's M-A-R-G-I-E.
BOY: And what is she in the film? I mean, what kind of person?
WOMAN: She's a cook. In the story she wants to be a singer but she hasn't got any money, so she has to work in a restaurant.
BOY: Oh, it sounds good. I'd like to see it now.
WOMAN: Yes. The actors were all excellent, and it's an interesting story too.

[pause]

Now listen to Part 2 again.

[The recording is repeated.]

[pause]

That is the end of Part 2.

[pause]

Part 3 *Listen and look. There is one example.*

[pause]

Peter has lots of friends who all do different jobs. Where did each of Peter's friends stay last summer?

[pause]

MAN: All my friends went to different places last summer. I've got one friend who's a journalist. He writes for an important newspaper and he works very hard. For his holidays last year, he stayed in a hotel near the beach and he didn't do any work!
WOMAN: That's good, Peter!

[pause]

Can you see the letter A? Now you listen and write a letter in each box.

[pause]

MAN: Another of my friends wanted a quiet holiday because she's got a busy job. She's a nurse in a big hospital. She stayed on a farm, but she didn't stay in the farmer's house because it was full. She slept in a tent in one of the fields there.
WOMAN: That's nice.

[pause]

WOMAN: What about your other friends?
MAN: Well, one of them sailed to a beautiful island. There were no hotels there so she slept on the boat. She's an artist and she paints pictures of the sea. She sells them for a lot of money.

[pause]

MAN: My best friend had a great holiday too. He's a dentist. He stayed in a forest and there were lots of birds and animals there, but only a few people. He slept each night in a little house made of wood.
WOMAN: And he wasn't afraid?
MAN: No!

[pause]

MAN: And I've got another friend who's a tennis player. She likes holidays in the mountains and she usually goes skiing, but last summer she wanted something different. She stayed in an old castle on top of a hill.
WOMAN: Did she show you some photos?

MAN: Yes. It looked lovely.

[pause]

MAN: And, oh, one more friend …
WOMAN: What does he do?
MAN: He's a teacher, and he loves visiting museums and going to the theatre, so he went to stay with his sister last summer because she's got an apartment in London. He enjoyed it a lot.
WOMAN: I'm not surprised. I'd like to do that too.

[pause]

Now listen to Part 3 again.

[The recording is repeated.]

[pause]

That is the end of Part 3.

[pause]

Part 4 *Listen and look. There is one example.*

[pause]

What does John like best at Century Park?

[pause]

WOMAN: What do you like best at Century Park, John?
BOY: Well, the lake is beautiful, with all the swans on it.
WOMAN: The pirate ship is good too.
BOY: Mmm … but it's only made of plastic. My favourite thing here is the little zoo.

[pause]

Can you see the tick? Now you listen and tick the box.

[pause]

1 Which T-shirt does John want?

WOMAN: Shall I buy this T-shirt for you, John?
BOY: Thanks, but I don't like the dinosaurs on the front.
WOMAN: Well, would you like this one with the different flags on it?
BOY: Yes, that's nice. I'd like that.
WOMAN: Or there's this blue and yellow one here.
BOY: Oh, no. I hate spots.

[pause]

2 What fruit is Mum eating?

BOY: Close your eyes and taste this fruit. What is it? Can you guess?
WOMAN: Mmm. It doesn't taste like pineapple. Is it mango, perhaps?
BOY: Wrong! Guess again.
WOMAN: It could be watermelon.
BOY: Right! Clever Mum!

[pause]

3 What time are they going to meet Aunt Emma?

WOMAN: We mustn't forget to meet Aunt Emma here this afternoon.
BOY: What time? Three o'clock?
WOMAN: Or half past three. I'm not sure.
BOY: We mustn't be late.
WOMAN: Wait, I wrote it in my diary. Here it is: 'a quarter to four'.

[pause]

4 Where are they going to meet Aunt Emma?

BOY: Where are we going to meet her?
WOMAN: In the restaurant, on the other side of the park.
BOY: Is it near the swings?
WOMAN: No, you go past them and over the bridge. Then it's straight on for half a kilometre …

[pause]

5 How is Aunt Emma going to get to Century Park?

BOY: How is Aunt Emma going to get here?
WOMAN: She'll come by bicycle.
BOY: But it's too far. She could take a taxi.
WOMAN: Not Aunt Emma!
BOY: She could catch a bus.
WOMAN: There are no buses to Century Park today.

[pause]

Now listen to Part 4 again.

[The recording is repeated.]

[pause]

That is the end of Part 4.

[pause]

Part 5 *Listen and look at the picture. There is one example.*

[pause]

MAN: Look at this picture.
GIRL: Yes. These two girls are in the kitchen.
MAN: Can you see the older one?
GIRL: Yes. She's writing a letter, isn't she?
MAN: That's right. Can you colour her hair brown?
GIRL: OK.

[pause]

Can you see the girl's brown hair? This is an example.
Now you listen and colour and write and draw.

[pause]

Test 3 Answers

1
MAN: Now can you colour the glass on the table?
GIRL: Which one?
MAN: The empty one.
GIRL: OK. Can I colour it orange?
MAN: Yes, that's fine.

[pause]

2
GIRL: Look, the children have done some drawings.
MAN: Yes, and someone has put them on the fridge door.
GIRL: Can I colour the octopus red?
MAN: No, I think green is better.
GIRL: OK.

[pause]

3
MAN: I'd like you to write something now. Can you see the date on the wall?
GIRL: Yes. It's the fifteenth.
MAN: Well, can you write the month under the number?
GIRL: All right. What shall I write?
MAN: Write 'April'.

[pause]

4
GIRL: Can I draw something now?
MAN: Yes, of course. Do you see the shelf?
GIRL: Which one – the higher one?
MAN: That's right. Draw a plate next to the bowl.
GIRL: On the right?
MAN: Yes, please. And colour it yellow.

[pause]

5
GIRL: Now can I colour the telephone on the wall?
MAN: No. I'd like you to colour one of the bins.
GIRL: Which one?
MAN: The metal one, near the cooker. Colour it blue.
GIRL: OK. I've finished now.

[pause]

Now listen to Part 5 again.

[The recording is repeated.]

[pause]

That is the end of the Flyers Practice Listening Test 3.

Reading and Writing

Part 1 (10 marks)

1 a waiter   2 vegetables   3 jam   4 tights
5 salt   6 a college   7 a belt   8 a factory
9 gloves   10 a secretary

Part 2 (7 marks)

1 no   2 no   3 no   4 yes   5 no
6 no   7 yes

Part 3 (5 marks)

1 F   2 H   3 B   4 E   5 A

Part 4 (6 marks)

1 running   2 lovely   3 mouth   4 piece
5 address   6 Fly and the bottle

Part 5 (7 marks)

1 leaves
2 (small) eggs
3 (the/William's/his) Grandpa/Grandfather/Grandad
4 grey and/& white // white and/& grey
5 (the/William's/his) Grandma/Grandmother/Grannie/Granny
6 car
7 (five/some) (little) (baby) birds

Part 6 (10 marks)

1 called   2 all   3 than   4 only   5 between
6 a   7 where   8 or   9 been   10 will

Part 7 (5 marks)

1 from   2 to   3 plays
4 going/planning   5 said

Speaking

Part	Examiner does this:	Examiner says this:	Minimum response expected from child:	Back-up questions:
	Usher brings candidate in.	Usher to examiner: **Hello, this is (child's name)***.		
		Examiner: **Hello, *. My name's *Jane/Ms Smith*.**	Hello.	
		What's your surname?	Silver	What's your family name?
		How old are you, *?	ten	Are you *ten*?
1	Shows candidate both **Find the Differences** pictures.	**Now, here are two pictures. My picture is nearly the same as yours, but some things are different.**		
	Points to the plants in each picture.	**For example, in my picture there are three plants, but in your picture there are four plants. OK?**		
		I'm going to say something about my picture. You tell me how your picture is different.		1. Point at relevant difference(s). 2. Repeat statement. 3. Ask back-up question.
	Describes things without pointing.	**In my picture, there are three children in bed. The boy is drinking.**	*In my picture, the boy's eating.*	Is the boy drinking?
		In my picture, it's half past four.	*In my picture, it's quarter past five.*	What time is it?
		In my picture, the doctor has got a blue torch/flashlight in his pocket.	*In my picture, he's got an orange torch/flashlight.*	What has the doctor got in his pocket?
		In my picture, I can see a computer on the desk.	*In my picture, I can't see a computer on the desk.*	Can you see a computer on the desk?
		In my picture, there's a girl with a broken arm. A woman is giving her a book.	*In my picture, she's giving her a comic.*	Is the woman giving the girl a book?
		In my picture, the toy truck is bigger than the toy train.	*In my picture, the train is bigger.*	Which toy is bigger?
2	Shows candidate both **film information pages**. Then points to candidate's information page.	**Paul and Vicky have both been to the cinema to see a film. I don't know anything about Paul's film, but you do. So I'm going to ask you some questions.**		
	Points to the boy on candidate's information page. Asks the questions.	**When did Paul see the film?**	*(on) Saturday*	Point at the information if necessary.
		Where is the cinema?	*(It's in) Market Street.*	
		Who did he go with?	*(his) uncle*	
		What's the name of the film?	*'The Black Pirate.'*	
		Is the film funny or sad?	*(It's) funny.*	

* Remember to use the child's name throughout the test.

Test 3 Answers

Part	Examiner does this:	Examiner says this:	Minimum response expected from child:	Back-up questions:
	Points to the girl on candidate's information page. Responds using information on examiner's information page.	Now you don't know anything about Vicky's film, so you ask me some questions. It's called 'The Blue Dolphin'. It's sad. on Friday She went with her grandmother. It's in Castle Road.	*What's the name of the film?* *Is the film funny or sad?* *When did Vicky see the film?* *Who did she go with?* *Where is the cinema?*	Point at information cues if necessary.
3	Shows candidate **Picture Story**. Allows time to look at the pictures.	These pictures tell a story. It's called 'Sam finds some treasure'. Just look at the pictures first. It's Sam's birthday today. His parents are giving him a present. Sam wants a drum. Now you tell the story.	 *Sam's opening his present. It's a rucksack. Sam isn't very happy.* *Sam is taking a map out of the rucksack. There's a red cross on it.* *Sam is walking round the garden.* *He's looking at the map.* *He's looking under a tree. There's a big drum.* *Sam is very happy.*	1. Point at the pictures. 2. Ask questions about the pictures. What's Sam's present? Is he happy? What has Sam found in the rucksack? Where is Sam now? What's he doing? What's under the tree? How does Sam feel now?
4	Puts the pictures away and turns to the candidate.	Now let's talk about your best friend. What's your best friend's name? How old is he/she? Where does he/she live? Is he/she tall or short? Tell me about the things you do with your best friend.	 *It's …* *(He/she's) 12.* *(He/she lives in) my street.* *(He/she's) tall.* *We go to school together.* *We play computer games.* *We go to the park.*	 Is your friend's name …? Is he/she 12? Does he/she live *in your street*? Is your friend *tall*? Do you *go to school* with your best friend? What do you do after school? Where do you go at the weekend?
		OK, thank you, *. Goodbye.	*Goodbye.*	

* Remember to use the child's name throughout the test.

COMBINED STARTERS, MOVERS AND FLYERS THEMATIC VOCABULARY LIST

For ease of reference, vocabulary is arranged in semantic groups or themes. Some words appear under more than one heading.

In addition to the topics, notions and concepts listed for the syllabus, the following categories appear:
- useful words and expressions
- adjectives
- determiners
- adverbs
- prepositions
- conjunctions
- pronouns
- verbs
- modals
- question words
- names

s – first appears at *Starters*
m – first appears at *Movers*
f – first appears at *Flyers*

ANIMALS

s	animal	f	insect	
m	bat	m	jungle	
m	bear	m	kangaroo	
s	bird	m	kitten	
f	butterfly	m	lion	
m	cage	s	lizard	
f	camel	s	monkey	
s	cat	s	mouse/mice	
s	chicken	f	octopus	
s	cow	m	panda	
s	crocodile	m	parrot	
f	dinosaur	m	pet	
s	dog	m	puppy	
m	dolphin	m	rabbit	
s	duck	m	shark	
s	elephant	s	sheep (s & pl)	
f	extinct	s	snake	
s	fish (s & pl)	s	spider	
m	fly	f	swan	
s	frog	s	tail	
f	fur	s	tiger	
s	giraffe	m	whale	
s	goat	f	wild	
s	hippo	f	wing	
s	horse	s	zoo	

THE BODY & FACE

s	arm	m	thin
m	back	f	toe
m	beard	m	tooth/teeth
m	blond(e)		
s	body	**CLOTHES**	
m	curly	s	bag
s	ear	f	belt
s	eye	s	clothes
s	face	m	coat
m	fair	f	crown
m	fat	s	dress
f	finger	s	glasses
s	foot/feet	f	glove
s	hair	s	handbag
s	hand	s	hat
s	head	s	jacket
s	leg	s	jeans
m	moustache	f	necklace
s	mouth	f	pocket
m	neck	f	ring
s	nose	m	scarf
m	shoulder	s	shirt
s	smile	s	shoe
m	stomach	f	shorts
m	straight		

25

Thematic Vocabulary List

- s skirt
- s sock
- f spot
- f spotted
- f stripe
- f striped
- f sunglasses
- m sweater
- f tights
- s trousers
- s T-shirt
- f umbrella
- f uniform
- s watch
- s wear

COLOURS

- s black
- s blue
- f bright (of colour)
- s brown
- s colour
- f gold
- s green
- s grey (US gray)
- s orange
- s pink
- s purple
- s red
- f silver
- s white
- s yellow

FAMILY & FRIENDS

- m aunt
- s baby
- s boy
- s brother
- s child/children
- s cousin
- s dad(dy)
- m daughter
- s family
- s father
- s friend
- f get married
- s girl
- m grandchild(ren)
- m granddaughter
- s grandfather
- s grandma
- s grandmother
- s grandpa
- m grandparent
- m grandson
- m grown-up
- f husband
- s live
- s man/men
- f married
- s Miss
- s mother
- s Mr
- s Mrs
- s mum(my) (US mom(my))
- s old
- m parent
- f partner
- s person/people
- s sister
- m son
- f surname
- m uncle
- f wife
- s woman/women
- s young

FOOD & DRINK

- s apple
- s banana
- s bean
- f biscuit (US cookie)
- m bottle
- m bowl
- s bread
- s breakfast
- s burger
- f butter
- s cake
- s candy (UK sweets)
- s carrot
- m cheese
- s chicken
- s chips (US fries)
- s chocolate
- f chopsticks
- s coconut
- m coffee
- f cookie (UK biscuit)
- m cup
- s dinner
- s drink (n & v)
- s eat
- s egg
- s fish
- f flour
- s food
- f fork
- s fries (UK chips)
- s fruit
- m glass (of)
- s grape
- f honey
- m hungry
- s ice cream
- f jam
- s juice
- f knife
- s lemon
- s lemonade
- s lime
- s lunch
- s mango
- f meal
- s meat
- s milk
- s onion
- s orange
- m pasta
- s pea
- s pear
- f pepper
- m picnic
- f piece
- s pineapple
- f pizza
- m plate
- s potato
- s rice
- m salad
- f salt
- m sandwich
- s sausage
- f smell
- s snack
- m soup
- f spoon
- f sugar
- s supper
- s sweets (US candy)
- f taste
- m tea
- m thirsty
- s tomato
- m vegetable
- s water
- s watermelon

HEALTH

- f chemist('s)
- m cold
- m cough
- m cry
- f cut
- f dentist
- m doctor
- m earache
- m fall
- f fall over
- m fine
- m headache
- m hospital
- m hurt
- f ill
- m matter (What's the matter?)
- f medicine
- m nurse
- f problem
- m stomach-ache
- m temperature
- m tired
- m toothache

THE HOME

- m address
- s apartment (UK flat)
- s armchair
- m balcony
- m basement
- s bath
- s bathroom
- s bed
- s bedroom
- m blanket
- s bookcase
- s box
- f brush
- s camera
- m CD player
- s chair
- s clock
- f comb
- s computer
- f cooker
- s cupboard
- s desk
- f diary
- s dining room
- s doll
- s door
- m downstairs
- m dream
- m DVD player
- m elevator (UK lift)
- f entrance
- f envelope
- m fan
- s flat (US apartment)
- s floor
- m floor (e.g. ground, 1st, etc.)
- s flower
- f fridge
- s garden
- f gate
- s hall

Thematic Vocabulary List

m	home
s	house
m	internet
f	key
s	kitchen
s	lamp
f	letter
m	lift (US elevator)
s	living room
s	mat
m	message
s	mirror
f	money
s	painting
s	phone
s	picture
s	radio
m	roof
s	room
f	screen
m	seat
s	secret
f	shelf
m	shopping
m	shower
s	sleep
f	soap
s	sofa
m	stair(s)
f	stamp
f	swing
s	table
f	telephone
s	television/TV
f	toilet
m	toothbrush
m	towel
s	toy
s	tree
m	upstairs
s	wall
m	wash (n&v)
s	watch
s	window

MATERIALS

f	card
f	glass
f	gold
f	metal
f	paper
f	plastic
f	silver
f	wood
f	wool

NUMBERS

s	Cardinals: 1–20
m	Cardinals: 21–100
f	Cardinals: 101–1000
m	hundred
f	million
m	Ordinals: 1st–20th
f	Ordinals: 21st–31st
m	pair
f	several
f	thousand

PLACES & DIRECTIONS

m	above
f	airport
m	bank
s	behind
m	below
s	between
s	bookshop
f	bridge
f	building
m	bus station
m	bus stop
m	café
f	castle
f	centimetre (US centimeter)
m	centre
f	chemist('s)
m	cinema
m	circle
f	circus
m	city/town centre
f	club
f	college
f	corner
f	east
f	end
f	factory
m	farm
f	fire station
f	front
f	get to
s	here
m	hospital
f	hotel
s	in
s	in front of
f	kilometre(s) (US kilometer(s))
f	left
m	library
f	London
m	map
m	market
f	metre (US meter)
f	middle
f	museum
m	near
s	next to
f	north
s	on
m	opposite
f	over
s	park
f	path
m	place
s	playground
f	police station
f	post office
f	restaurant
f	right
m	road
s	shop (US store)
m	shopping centre
f	south
m	sports centre
m	square
m	station
s	store (UK shop)
m	straight
f	straight on
s	street
m	supermarket
m	swimming pool
f	theatre
s	there
m	town/city centre
s	under
f	university
f	way
f	west
s	zoo

SCHOOL

s	alphabet
s	answer
f	art
s	ask
f	backpack (UK rucksack)
f	bin
s	board
s	book
s	bookcase
m	break
s	class
s	classroom
s	close
f	club
f	college
s	colour
f	competition
s	computer
s	correct
s	cross
s	cupboard
s	desk
f	dictionary
s	door
s	draw(ing)
s	English
s	eraser (UK rubber)
f	exam (examination)
s	example
f	fact
s	find
f	flag
s	floor
f	geography
f	glue
f	group
f	headteacher
f	history
m	homework
m	internet
s	keyboard (computer)
s	know
f	language
s	learn
s	lesson
s	letter (as in alphabet)
s	line
s	listen (to)
s	look
f	maths (US math)
m	mistake
s	mouse (computer)
s	music
s	name
s	number
f	online
s	open
s	page
s	part
s	pen
s	pencil
s	picture
s	playground
s	question
s	read
s	right (as in correct)
s	rubber (US eraser)
f	rucksack (US backpack)
s	ruler
s	school
f	science
f	scissors
f	screen
s	sentence
f	shelf

Thematic Vocabulary List

s	sit
s	spell
s	stand (up)
s	story
f	student
f	study
f	subject
f	teach
s	teacher
s	tell
s	test (n & v)
m	text
s	tick (n & v)
f	timetable
s	understand
f	university
s	wall
m	website
s	window
s	word
s	write
f	zero

SPORTS & LEISURE

f	backpack (UK rucksack)
s	badminton
s	ball
m	band (music)
s	baseball
s	basketball
m	bat
s	beach
s	bike
s	boat
s	book
s	bounce
s	camera
f	cartoon
s	catch
m	CD
m	CD player
f	channel
f	chess
f	collect
m	comic/comic book
f	concert
f	conversation
m	dance
f	diary
s	doll
s	draw(ing)
m	drive (n)
s	drive (v)
f	drum
m	DVD
m	DVD player
m	email
s	enjoy
s	favourite
m	film (US movie)
m	fish (v)
s	fish(ing)
f	flashlight (UK torch)
s	fly
s	football (US soccer)
s	game
f	goal
m	go shopping
f	golf
s	guitar
s	hit
s	hobby
s	hockey
m	holiday
m	hop
f	hotel
f	instrument
f	join (a club)
s	jump
m	kick (n)
s	kick (v)
s	kite
s	listen (to)
f	magazine
f	match
f	meet
f	member
m	movie (UK film)
s	music
f	online
s	paint(ing)
m	party
s	photo
s	piano
s	picture
s	play (with)
f	player (as in CD player)
m	pool
f	postcard
m	present
f	prize
f	programme (US program)
f	race
s	radio
s	read
m	ride (n)
s	ride (v)
f	rucksack (US backpack)
s	run
m	sail
f	score
s	sing
m	skate
f	ski
m	skip
f	sledge
f	snowball
f	snowboarding
f	snowman
s	soccer (UK football)
s	song
s	sport
m	sports centre
f	stage (theatre)
s	story
f	suitcase
m	swim (n)
s	swim (v)
m	swimming pool
f	swing
s	table tennis
s	take a photo/picture
f	tape recorder
s	team
s	television/TV
s	tennis
f	tent
m	text (n & v)
s	throw
f	torch (US flashlight)
m	towel
s	toy
s	TV/television
f	umbrella
m	video
f	violin
f	volleyball
m	walk (n)
s	walk (v)
s	watch
f	winner

TIME

f	a.m.
m	after
s	afternoon
m	age
f	ago
m	always
f	autumn (US fall)
m	before
s	birthday
f	calendar
f	century
f	Christmas
s	clock
f	date
s	day
f	early
s	end
s	evening
m	every
f	fall (UK autumn)
f	future
f	half
f	hour
f	how long
f	late
f	later
f	midday
f	midnight
f	minute
f	month
s	morning
m	never
s	night
f	o'clock
f	p.m.
f	past
f	quarter
m	sometimes
f	spring
f	summer
f	time
s	today
f	tomorrow
f	tonight
s	watch
m	week
m	weekend
f	winter
s	year
m	yesterday

The days of the week:

m	Sunday
m	Monday
m	Tuesday
m	Wednesday
m	Thursday
m	Friday
m	Saturday

The months of the year:

f	January
f	February
f	March
f	April
f	May
f	June
f	July
f	August
f	September
f	October
f	November
f	December

TOYS

s	alien
s	ball
s	balloon
s	baseball

Thematic Vocabulary List

- s basketball
- s bike
- s boat
- s car
- f crown
- s doll
- s football (US soccer)
- s game
- s helicopter
- s kite
- s lorry (US truck)
- s monster
- s plane
- s robot
- s soccer (UK football)
- s toy
- s train
- m treasure
- s truck (UK lorry)

TRANSPORT

- f airport
- f ambulance
- f bicycle
- s bike
- s boat
- s bus
- m bus station
- m bus stop
- s car
- m drive (n)
- s drive (v)
- m driver
- f fire engine (US fire truck)
- s fly (v)
- s go
- s helicopter
- f journey
- f lift (US ride)
- s lorry (US truck)
- s motorbike
- f passenger
- s plane
- f railway
- m ride (n)
- s ride (v)
- f rocket
- s run
- m station
- s swim
- f taxi
- m ticket
- f timetable
- f tour
- f traffic
- s train
- m trip
- s truck (UK lorry)
- s walk (n)
- m walk (v)
- f wheel

WEATHER

- m cloud
- m cloudy
- f fog
- f foggy
- f ice
- m rain
- m rainbow
- f sky
- m snow
- f storm
- s sun
- m sunny
- m weather
- m wind
- m windy

WORK

- f actor/actress
- f airport
- f ambulance
- f artist
- f astronaut
- f business
- f businessman/woman
- f circus
- m clown
- f cook
- f dentist
- m doctor
- m driver
- f engineer
- f factory
- m farmer
- f fireman/woman
- f footballer
- m hospital
- f job
- f journalist
- f mechanic
- f meeting
- f news
- f newspaper
- f nurse
- f office
- f painter
- f photographer
- f pilot
- m pirate
- f police station
- f policeman/woman
- f queen
- f secretary
- f singer
- f taxi
- s teacher
- f tennis player
- f waiter
- m work

THE WORLD AROUND US

- f air
- s beach
- f bridge
- f building
- f castle
- f cave
- m city
- m country(side)
- f desert
- f entrance
- f environment
- f exit
- m field
- f fire
- m forest
- f future
- f gate
- m grass
- m ground
- f hill
- m island
- m jungle
- m lake
- m leaf/leaves
- m moon
- m mountain
- f planet
- m plant
- f pyramid
- m river
- m road
- m rock
- s sand
- s sea
- s shell
- f sky
- f space
- m star
- s street
- s sun
- m town
- s tree
- f view
- m village
- s water
- m waterfall
- f wood
- m world

USEFUL WORDS & EXPRESSIONS

- s bye (-bye)
- m come on!
- f excellent
- m excuse me
- s goodbye
- s hello
- s I don't know
- s no
- s oh
- s oh dear
- s OK
- s pardon
- s please
- s right
- m see you!
- s so
- s sorry
- s thank you
- s thanks
- s then
- s well
- s well done
- s wow!
- s yes

ADJECTIVES

- m afraid
- m all
- m all right
- f alone
- s angry
- m awake
- m back
- m bad
- s beautiful
- m best
- m better
- s big
- m blond(e)
- f bored
- m boring
- m bottom
- f brave
- f bright (of colour)
- f broken
- m busy
- m careful
- f cheap
- s clean
- m clever
- s closed
- m cloudy
- m cold
- s correct
- m curly

Thematic Vocabulary List

f	dangerous	f	light	m	surprised		**ADVERBS**
f	dark	f	little	m	sweet	f	a little
f	dear	s	long	m	tall	s	a lot
m	different	m	loud	m	terrible	f	actually
m	difficult	f	lovely	s	their	f	after
s	dirty	f	low	m	thin	s	again
s	double	f	lucky	m	third	f	ago
m	dry	f	many	m	thirsty	m	all
f	early	f	married	f	tidy	m	all right
m	easy	f	metal	m	tired	f	already
f	empty	f	middle	m	top	f	also
s	English	f	missing	s	ugly	m	always
f	enough	m	more	f	unfriendly	f	anywhere
m	every	m	most	f	unhappy	f	away
f	excellent	s	my	f	untidy	m	back
f	excited	m	naughty	f	unusual	m	badly
m	exciting	s	new	f	warm	f	before
f	expensive	f	next	m	weak	m	best
f	extinct	s	nice	m	well	m	better
m	fair	f	noisy	m	wet	m	carefully
m	famous	s	OK	f	wild	m	down
f	far	s	old	m	windy	m	downstairs
f	fast	f	online	f	wonderful	f	early
m	fat	s	open	f	worried	f	else
s	favourite	f	other	m	worse	f	ever
m	fine	s	our	m	worst	f	everywhere
m	first	f	paper	m	wrong	f	far
f	foggy	f	plastic	s	young	f	fast
f	friendly	f	poor	s	your	m	first
m	frightened	f	popular			f	hard
f	front	m	pretty		**DETERMINERS**	s	here
f	full	m	quick	s	a/an	s	home
f	fun	m	quiet	f	a few	m	how
s	funny	f	ready	f	a little	f	how long
f	glass	f	rich	s	a lot of	m	how much
f	gold	s	right (correct)	m	all	m	how often
s	good	f	right (as in direction)	m	another	m	inside
s	great	m	round	m	any	f	just
f	half	s	sad	m	both	m	last
s	happy	m	safe	f	each	f	late
f	hard	f	same	m	every	f	later
f	heavy	m	second	s	lots of	s	lots
s	her	s	short	s	many	m	loudly
f	high	f	silver	m	more	m	more
s	his	f	single	m	most	m	most
f	horrible	m	slow	f	much	f	much
m	hot	s	small	s	my	m	near
m	hungry	f	soft	s	no	m	never
f	ill	s	sorry	s	one	f	next
f	important	f	special	f	other	s	no
f	interesting	f	spotted	s	some	s	not
s	its	m	square	f	such	s	now
f	kind	m	straight	s	that	f	nowhere
f	large	f	strange	s	the	f	o'clock
m	last	f	striped	s	these	f	of course (not)
f	late	m	strong	s	this	m	off
f	lazy	m	sunny	s	those	m	often
f	left (as in direction)	f	sure				

Thematic Vocabulary List

m	on	*f*	for (prep of time)	*s*	hers	*s*	drink
f	once	*s*	from	*f*	herself	*s*	drive
m	only	*s*	in (prep of place)	*s*	him	*m*	dry
m	out	*m*	in (prep of time)	*f*	himself	*s*	eat
m	outside	*s*	in front of	*s*	his	*m*	fall
f	over	*m*	inside	*s*	I	*f*	fall over
f	perhaps	*m*	into	*s*	it	*f*	feel (like)
m	quickly	*s*	like	*s*	its	*s*	find
m	quietly	*m*	near	*f*	itself	*f*	find out
f	quite	*s*	next to	*s*	lots	*s*	fly
s	really	*s*	of	*s*	me	*f*	forget
m	round	*m*	off	*s*	mine	*s*	get
m	second	*s*	on (prep of place)	*m*	more	*f*	get (to)
m	slowly	*m*	on (prep of time)	*m*	most	*m*	get (un)dressed
f	so	*m*	opposite	*f*	much	*m*	get (up/on/off)
m	sometimes	*m*	out of	*f*	myself	*s*	give
f	somewhere	*m*	outside	*f*	no-one	*s*	go
f	soon	*f*	over	*m*	nothing	*f*	go out
f	still	*f*	past	*s*	one	*m*	go shopping
f	straight on	*m*	round	*f*	other	*f*	grow
f	suddenly	*f*	since	*s*	ours	*s*	have
s	then	*m*	than	*s*	she	*s*	have (got)
s	there	*f*	through	*m*	someone	*m*	have (got) to
m	third	*s*	to	*m*	something	*f*	hear
s	today	*s*	under	*s*	that	*m*	hide
f	together	*m*	up	*s*	theirs	*s*	hit
f	tomorrow	*f*	until	*s*	them	*s*	hold
f	tonight	*s*	with	*s*	these	*m*	hurt
s	too	*f*	without	*s*	they	*f*	keep
f	twice			*s*	this	*s*	know
m	up	**CONJUNCTIONS**		*s*	those	*s*	learn
m	upstairs	*f*	after	*s*	us	*f*	leave
f	usually	*s*	and	*s*	we	*f*	let
s	very	*m*	because	*f*	where	*s*	let's
m	well	*f*	before	*m*	which	*f*	lie (down)
m	when	*s*	but	*m*	who	*m*	lose
m	worse	*f*	if	*s*	you	*s*	make
m	worst	*s*	or	*s*	yours	*f*	make sure
s	yes	*f*	so	*f*	yourself	*m*	mean
m	yesterday	*m*	than			*f*	meet
f	yet	*m*	when	**VERBS**		*s*	put
				Irregular:		*m*	put on
PREPOSITIONS		**PRONOUNS**		*s*	be	*s*	read
s	about	*s*	a lot	*m*	be called	*s*	ride
m	above	*m*	all	*f*	be going to	*s*	run
f	across	*m*	another	*f*	begin	*s*	say
m	after	*m*	any	*f*	break	*s*	see
s	at (prep of place)	*f*	anyone	*m*	bring	*f*	sell
m	at (prep of time)	*f*	anything	*f*	burn	*f*	send
m	before	*m*	both	*m*	buy	*s*	sing
s	behind	*f*	each	*s*	catch (a ball)	*s*	sit (down)
m	below	*f*	else	*m*	catch (a bus)	*s*	sleep
s	between	*f*	enough	*s*	choose	*f*	smell (v intr)
m	by	*m*	everyone	*s*	come	*f*	smell (like) (v tr)
m	down	*m*	everything	*f*	cut	*f*	speak
f	during	*s*	he	*s*	do	*s*	spell
s	for	*s*	her	*s*	draw	*f*	spend
						s	stand (up)

31

Thematic Vocabulary List

f	steal	f	guess	f	stay		**NAMES**
s	swim	f	happen	s	stop	s	Alex
f	swing	f	hate	f	study	s	Ann
m	take	m	help	s	talk	s	Anna
m	take (a bus)	m	hop	f	taste (like)	s	Ben
s	take (a photo)	f	hope	s	test	f	Betty
m	take off	f	hurry	m	text	s	Bill
f	take (time)	f	improve	f	thank	m	Charlie
f	teach	m	invite	s	tick	m	Daisy
s	tell	f	join (a club)	f	tidy	s	Dan
m	think	s	jump	m	travel	f	David
s	throw	s	kick	s	try	f	Emma
s	understand	m	laugh	f	turn	m	Fred
m	wake up	s	learn	f	turn (off/on)	f	George
s	wear	f	lift	f	use	s	Grace
f	win	s	like	m	video	f	Harry
s	write	s	listen (to)	f	visit	f	Helen
		s	live	m	wait	f	Holly
	Regular:	s	look	s	walk	m	Jack
s	add	f	look after	s	want	m	Jane
f	agree	s	look at	m	wash	s	Jill
s	answer	m	look for	s	watch	m	Jim
f	arrive	f	look (like)	s	wave	m	John
s	ask	s	love	f	whisper	f	Katy
f	believe	f	mind	f	whistle	s	Kim
s	bounce	f	mix	f	wish	m	Lily
f	brush	m	move	m	work	s	Lucy
f	burn	m	need			m	Mary
m	call	s	open		**MODALS**	s	May
f	camp	s	paint	s	can/cannot/can't	f	Michael
m	carry	s	phone	m	could (past ability)	s	Nick
m	change	s	pick up	f	could (possibility)	s	Pat
s	clean	m	plant	f	may	m	Paul
m	climb	s	play (with)	f	might	m	Peter
s	close	s	point (to)	m	must	f	Richard
f	collect	f	post	m	shall	f	Robert
s	colour	f	prefer	f	should	m	Sally
f	comb	f	pull	f	will	s	Sam
s	complete	f	push	m	would	f	Sarah
m	cook	f	race			s	Sue
s	cross	m	rain		**QUESTION WORDS**	s	Tom
m	cry	f	remember	s	how	s	Tony
m	dance	f	repair	f	how long	m	Vicky
f	decide	f	repeat	s	how many	f	William
f	describe	m	sail	m	how much		
m	dream	f	save	f	how often		
m	dress up	f	score	s	how old		
m	drop	m	shop	s	what		
m	email	m	shout	m	when		
f	end	s	show	s	where		
s	enjoy	m	skate	s	which		
f	explain	f	ski	s	who		
f	fetch	m	skip	s	whose		
m	film	f	sledge	m	why		
f	finish	s	smile				
m	fish	m	snow				
f	follow	f	sound (like)				
f	glue	s	start				

Thematic Vocabulary List

m	on	*f*	for (prep of time)	*s*	hers	*s*	drink
f	once	*s*	from	*f*	herself	*s*	drive
m	only	*s*	in (prep of place)	*s*	him	*m*	dry
m	out	*m*	in (prep of time)	*f*	himself	*s*	eat
m	outside	*s*	in front of	*s*	his	*m*	fall
f	over	*m*	inside	*s*	I	*f*	fall over
f	perhaps	*m*	into	*s*	it	*f*	feel (like)
m	quickly	*s*	like	*s*	its	*s*	find
m	quietly	*m*	near	*f*	itself	*f*	find out
f	quite	*s*	next to	*s*	lots	*s*	fly
s	really	*s*	of	*s*	me	*f*	forget
m	round	*m*	off	*s*	mine	*s*	get
m	second	*s*	on (prep of place)	*m*	more	*f*	get (to)
m	slowly	*m*	on (prep of time)	*m*	most	*m*	get (un)dressed
f	so	*m*	opposite	*f*	much	*m*	get (up/on/off)
m	sometimes	*m*	out of	*f*	myself	*s*	give
f	somewhere	*m*	outside	*f*	no-one	*s*	go
f	soon	*f*	over	*m*	nothing	*f*	go out
f	still	*f*	past	*s*	one	*m*	go shopping
f	straight on	*m*	round	*f*	other	*f*	grow
f	suddenly	*f*	since	*s*	ours	*s*	have
s	then	*m*	than	*s*	she	*s*	have (got)
s	there	*f*	through	*m*	someone	*m*	have (got) to
m	third	*s*	to	*m*	something	*f*	hear
s	today	*s*	under	*s*	that	*m*	hide
f	together	*m*	up	*s*	theirs	*s*	hit
f	tomorrow	*f*	until	*s*	them	*s*	hold
f	tonight	*s*	with	*s*	these	*m*	hurt
s	too	*f*	without	*s*	they	*f*	keep
f	twice			*s*	this	*s*	know
m	up	**CONJUNCTIONS**		*s*	those	*s*	learn
m	upstairs	*f*	after	*s*	us	*f*	leave
f	usually	*s*	and	*s*	we	*f*	let
s	very	*m*	because	*f*	where	*s*	let's
m	well	*f*	before	*m*	which	*f*	lie (down)
m	when	*s*	but	*m*	who	*m*	lose
m	worse	*f*	if	*s*	you	*s*	make
m	worst	*s*	or	*s*	yours	*f*	make sure
s	yes	*f*	so	*f*	yourself	*m*	mean
m	yesterday	*m*	than			*f*	meet
f	yet	*m*	when	**VERBS**		*s*	put
				Irregular:		*m*	put on
PREPOSITIONS		**PRONOUNS**		*s*	be	*s*	read
s	about	*s*	a lot	*m*	be called	*s*	ride
m	above	*m*	all	*f*	be going to	*s*	run
f	across	*m*	another	*f*	begin	*s*	say
m	after	*m*	any	*f*	break	*s*	see
s	at (prep of place)	*f*	anyone	*f*	burn	*f*	sell
m	at (prep of time)	*f*	anything	*m*	bring	*f*	send
m	before	*m*	both	*m*	buy	*s*	sing
s	behind	*f*	each	*s*	catch (a ball)	*s*	sit (down)
m	below	*f*	else	*m*	catch (a bus)	*s*	sleep
s	between	*f*	enough	*s*	choose	*f*	smell (v intr)
m	by	*m*	everyone	*s*	come	*f*	smell (like) (v tr)
m	down	*m*	everything	*f*	cut	*f*	speak
f	during	*s*	he	*s*	do	*s*	spell
s	for	*s*	her	*s*	draw	*f*	spend
						s	stand (up)

Thematic Vocabulary List

f	steal	f	guess	f	stay	**NAMES**	
s	swim	f	happen	s	stop	s	Alex
f	swing	f	hate	f	study	s	Ann
m	take	m	help	s	talk	s	Anna
m	take (a bus)	m	hop	f	taste (like)	s	Ben
s	take (a photo)	f	hope	s	test	f	Betty
m	take off	f	hurry	m	text	s	Bill
f	take (time)	f	improve	f	thank	m	Charlie
f	teach	m	invite	s	tick	m	Daisy
s	tell	f	join (a club)	f	tidy	s	Dan
m	think	s	jump	m	travel	f	David
s	throw	s	kick	s	try	f	Emma
s	understand	m	laugh	f	turn	m	Fred
m	wake up	s	learn	f	turn (off/on)	f	George
s	wear	f	lift	f	use	s	Grace
f	win	s	like	m	video	f	Harry
s	write	s	listen (to)	f	visit	f	Helen
		s	live	m	wait	f	Holly
Regular:		s	look	s	walk	m	Jack
s	add	f	look after	s	want	m	Jane
f	agree	s	look at	m	wash	s	Jill
s	answer	m	look for	s	watch	m	Jim
f	arrive	f	look (like)	s	wave	m	John
s	ask	s	love	f	whisper	f	Katy
f	believe	f	mind	f	whistle	s	Kim
s	bounce	f	mix	f	wish	m	Lily
f	brush	m	move	m	work	s	Lucy
f	burn	m	need			m	Mary
m	call	s	open	**MODALS**		s	May
f	camp	s	paint	s	can/cannot/can't	f	Michael
m	carry	s	phone	m	could (past ability)	s	Nick
m	change	s	pick up	f	could (possibility)	s	Pat
s	clean	m	plant	f	may	m	Paul
m	climb	s	play (with)	f	might	m	Peter
s	close	s	point (to)	m	must	f	Richard
f	collect	f	post	m	shall	f	Robert
s	colour	f	prefer	f	should	m	Sally
f	comb	f	pull	f	will	s	Sam
s	complete	f	push	m	would	f	Sarah
m	cook	f	race			s	Sue
s	cross	m	rain	**QUESTION WORDS**		s	Tom
m	cry	f	remember	s	how	s	Tony
m	dance	f	repair	f	how long	m	Vicky
f	decide	f	repeat	s	how many	f	William
f	describe	m	sail	m	how much		
m	dream	f	save	f	how often		
m	dress up	f	score	s	how old		
m	drop	m	shop	s	what		
m	email	m	shout	m	when		
f	end	s	show	s	where		
s	enjoy	m	skate	s	which		
f	explain	f	ski	s	who		
f	fetch	m	skip	s	whose		
m	film	f	sledge	m	why		
f	finish	s	smile				
m	fish	m	snow				
f	follow	f	sound (like)				
f	glue	s	start				